1983

MEET CAMILLE AND DANILLE
they are special persons

by Margaret H. Glazzard, Ed.D.

in cooperation with:

Dr. Raymond D. Wair, Superintendent of Schools
North Kansas City School District 74

Dr. John W. DeArman, Assistant Superintendent of
Schools for Instruction
North Kansas City School District 74

Mr. Carl Thompson, Principal
Gashland School
North Kansas City School District 74

Mrs. Karen Crownover, Kindergarten Teacher
Gashland School
North Kansas City School District 74

**Special Consultant for Meet Camille & Danille -
They're Special Persons:**

Dr. Al Larson, Associate Professor of Deaf Education
University of Kansas

A special thanks to Phyllis Rogoff for
help with the manuscript.

photography by Hank Young: Young/Craig Photography
design by David Graves
printing by Meseraull Printing, Inc

H & H Enterprises, Inc.
Box 1070
Lawrence, Kansas 66044

First published in the United States of America in 1978 by H & H Enterprises, Inc. Box 1070, Lawrence, Kansas 66044.

ISBN: 0-89079-037-X

Foreword

This "Meet" series is the culmination of a four-year effort to prepare materials to explain handicapped youngsters to normal youngsters who may be in the same classroom or in the same school. By doing this at an early age we can help prevent prejudice and the use of derisive terms that often surface at a later age. Such prejudice and labeling are the result of a lack of understanding of handicaps.

I have tried to state the differences between handicapped and normal children while stressing that all children are more alike than they are different from each other. I also tried to show the types of curricula that handicapped children may need during their school day, and what normal children can do if a child with a particular handicap is a classmate.

Part of the vocabulary may be difficult for some early readers. To help overcome this, I have listed new words in the order they appear by page number at the end of the book. Correct vocabulary should be taught from the beginning when discussing handicapped children. This avoids slang terms that may become as popular as they are cruel.

Readability formulas have been applied to the text of each book and all books have been field-tested with second and third grade readers. Fry Readability Formula Graph—middle second grade (2M), and Spache Readability Formula—3.2 grade level, for this book. The story records make it possible for preschool and other beginning readers to use the books.

Margaret H. Glazzard, Ed.D.

Dedication

This book is dedicated to the Deaf Pre-School in the Children's Rehabilitation Unit, University of Kansas Medical Center. The pre-school plays a vital part in preparing many hearing handicapped youngsters to enter regular education classes. Camille and Danille attended the pre-school.

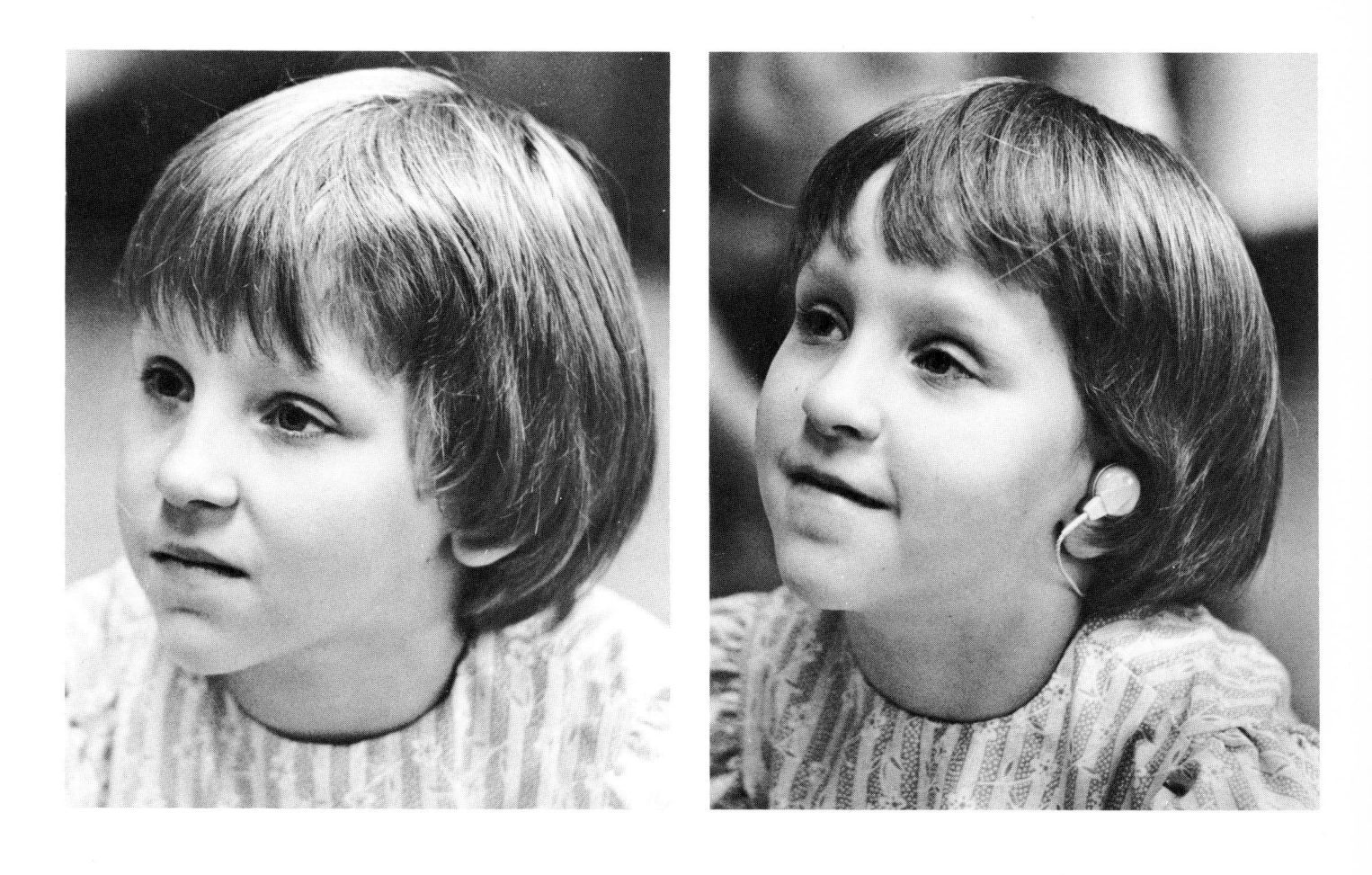

MEET CAMILLE AND DANILLE
they are special persons

Camille and Danille are twins. They are special because they cannot hear with their ears like you do. They are sometimes called "deaf" or "hearing impaired." This means not hearing very well or not hearing at all.

The twins are in a class with boys and girls who can hear. They like to play alphabet bingo. They can see the letters as they are called out.

Both girls wear hearing aids. A hearing aid is like a tiny radio. Sounds go into this tiny radio through a speaker. The hearing aid makes the sounds much louder. But even a hearing aid cannot help the girls hear as well as other boys and girls.

Z

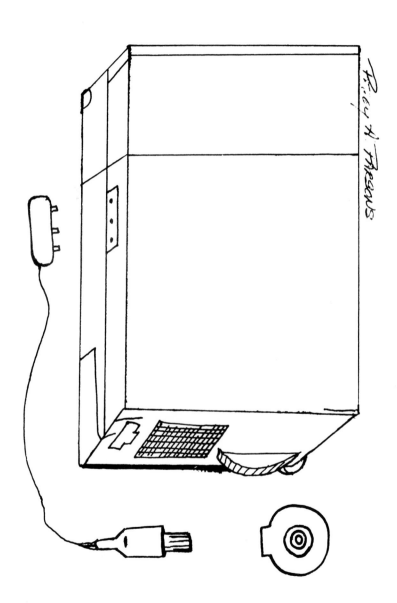

Camille wears a body hearing aid. She wears it on her chest. She shows it to her friends. Now they will know about hearing aids.

Danille wears another kind of hearing aid. It is called an ear level aid. She wears it behind her ear. It looks like a half-moon.   Hearing aids make the sounds louder but the girls must learn what these new sounds mean.

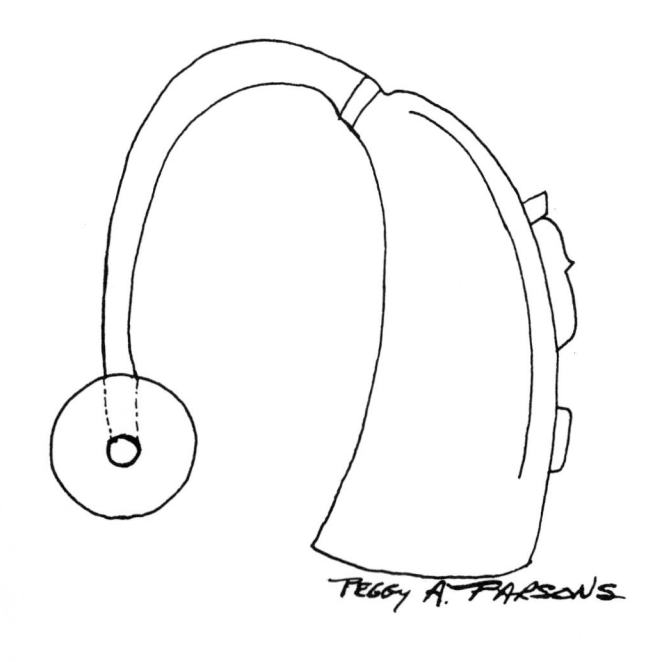

11

Getting a drink is fun but Camille and Danille must be more careful. Hearing aids, like radios, must not get wet.

The twins have learned to **see** words that people say. This is called "speech-reading." Lips move in a different way for each word we say. If you watch very carefully, you can tell what the word is by the way the lips move.

Look in a mirror and say, "baby." Now say "car." Can you see that your lips do not look the same? Some words are very hard to see because they look alike.

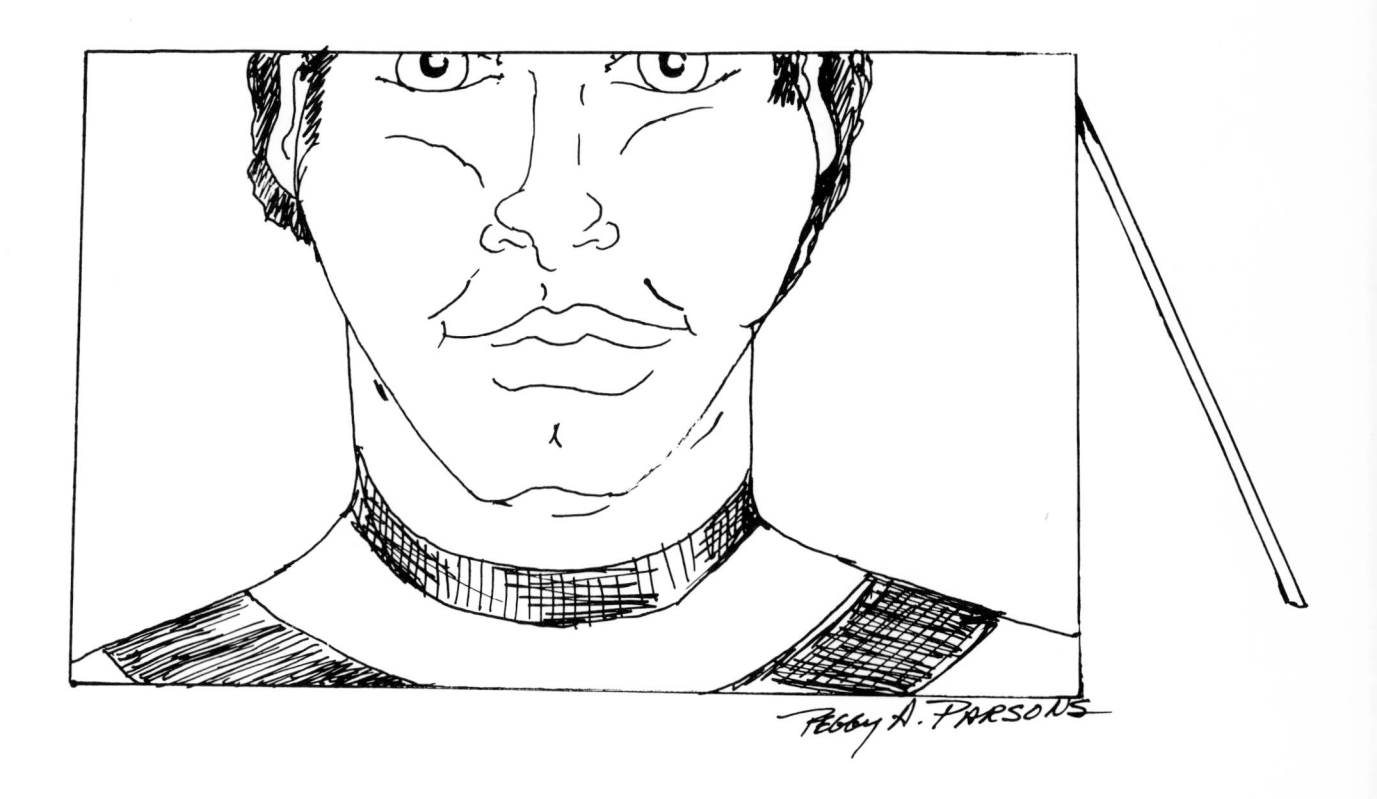

John looks in a mirror to say "man," "pan." It looks like his lips move the same. Some words look alike when you say them.

19

The girls must watch their teacher's face and lips. They must see how words look when she reads a story. Their hearing aids help but they must use their eyes, too.

Mrs. King must hold her book away from her face. She knows that the twins must see her lips when she reads or talks.

Hearing impaired children cannot see lips moving if the sun is shining in their eyes. Danille keeps her back to the window. She can see other faces better that way.

25

The teacher has put names on things in the classroom. The names help the twins to learn new words. The girls now know what the new words mean. Can you read the words? That's right. They say, "Sink," "Pencil Sharpener" and "Record Player."

Camille's friend taps her on the back. He knows that Camille must look at him. She must see his lips when he talks.

The teacher puts notes about class trips on the bulletin board. Children who do not hear must see these notes. Danille and Camille's class is going to the zoo. The note tells them about the trip so they will not forget.

It is hard to learn to talk when you can't hear. Camille has learned to **feel** words. Put your hand on your neck and say, "run." Do you feel your neck move? Now say, "skipping." Does it move the same? Different words make your neck move in different ways. When Camille talks, she may not sound the same as you. She must learn to talk by seeing and feeling because she cannot hear the sounds.

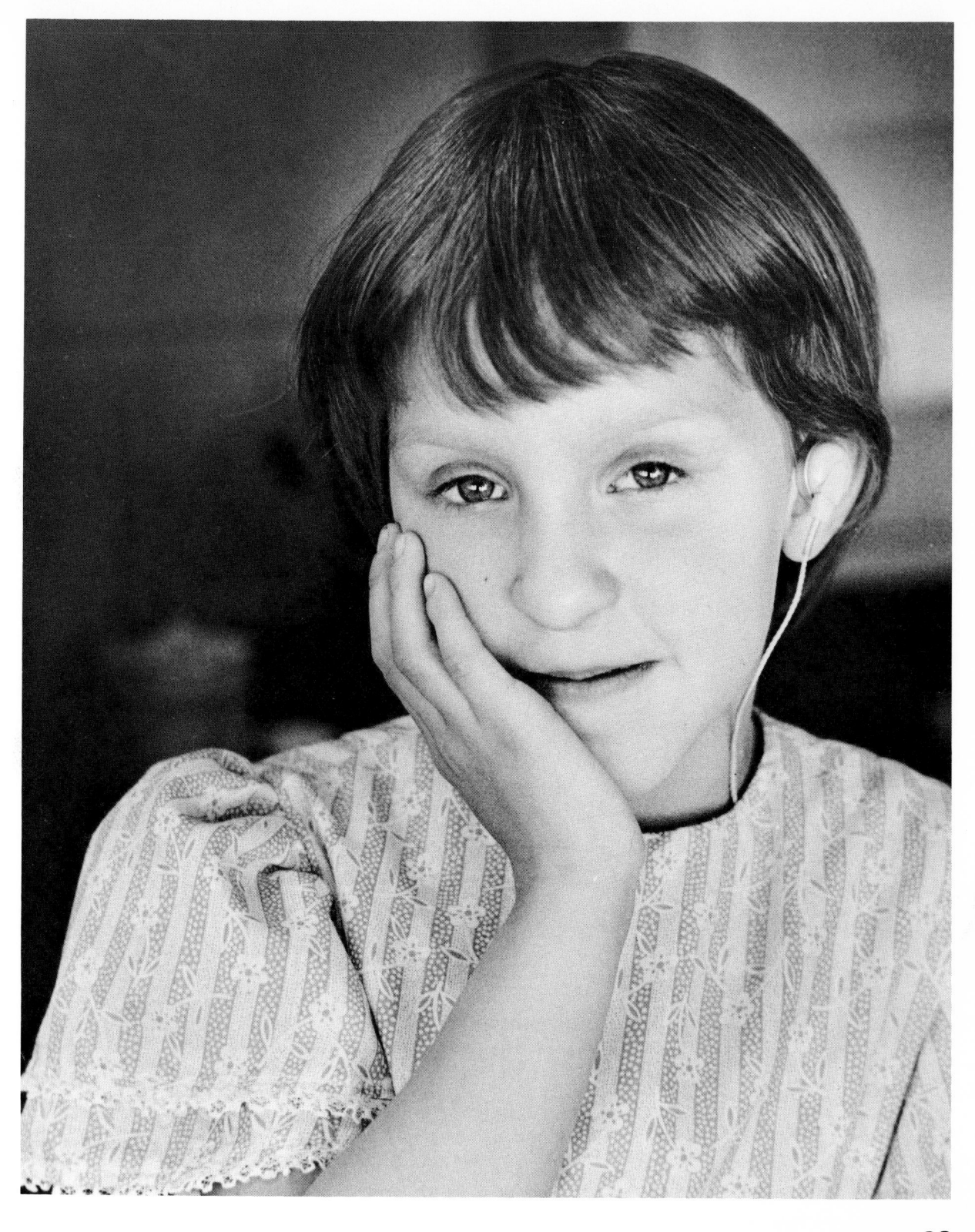

The girls like to talk at recess. Other girls do not whisper. They know that Camille and Danille cannot hear them. The twins would be unhappy if they missed what was said.

The teacher uses pictures when she teaches the class. Pictures help the twins see what the teacher is talking about.

red
blue
green
orange
brown
black
yellow

circle
triangle
square
rectangle
oval
diamond
half circle

A child who cannot hear should have a "buddy." The buddy can show the child around the school and the playground. Danille has fun running with her "buddy."

The twins like to play singing games with their friends just like you do. Can you guess what they are singing? They are singing "Where is Thumbkin?" and "Eeensy Weensy Spider."

Looking at people talk when you cannot hear them is hard work. The girls get very tired. Sometimes they need to rest just like you.

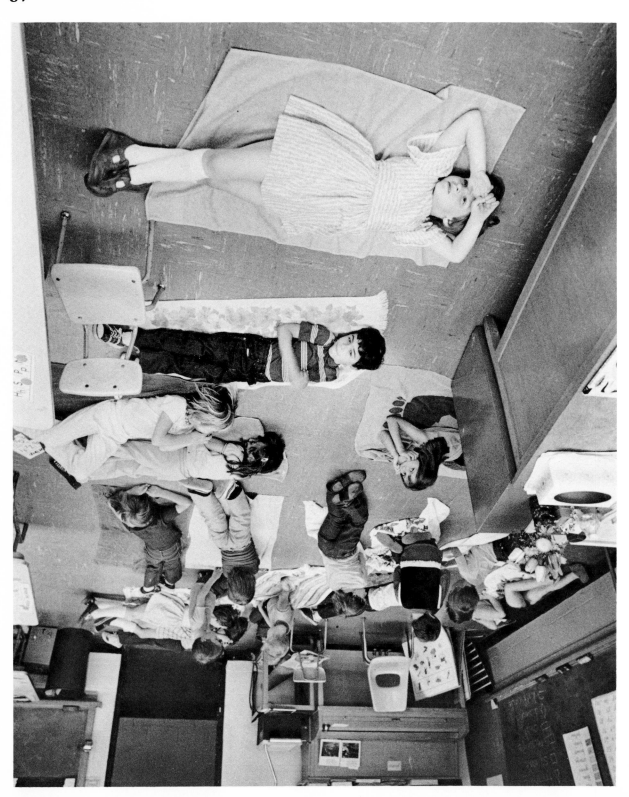

When you talk to children who cannot hear, talk as you always do. Do not speak too slowly or too fast.

When you invite children who cannot hear to a party, write them an invitation. Do not call on the telephone. They might not know what you want. An invitation helps them to remember the day and the time.

Camille and Danille like to play just like you. They can run and jump and laugh just like you. They must work harder to learn to talk and read and write because they cannot hear as you do. The girls are smart and they can learn. Aren't you glad you met Camille and Danille? They are very special children!

Meet Camille and Danille - They're Special Persons

Vocabulary as introduced:

Page 2	**Page 2**	**Page 4**	**Page 6**
Camille	means	the	both
and	not	in	wear
Danille	very	a	aids
are	well	class	aid
twins	at	boys	is
they	all	girls	tiny
special		who	radio
because		can	sounds
cannot		to	go
hear		play	into
with		alphabet	through
their		bingo	speaker
ears		see	makes
like		letters	much
you		as	louder
do		out	but
sometimes			even
called			help
deaf			other
or			
hearing			
impaired			
this			

Page 8	**Page 10**	**Page 12**	**Page 14**
wears	another	getting	have
body	kind	drink	learned
she	of	fun	words
it	an	be	that
on	ear	more	people
her	level	careful	say
chest	behind	radios	speech
shows	looks	get	reading
friends	half-moon	wet	lips
now	make		move
will	must		different
know	learn		way
about	what		for
	these		each
	new		word
	mean		we
			if
			watch
			carefully
			tell
			by

Page 16
your
same
some
hard
alike
look
mirror
baby
car

Page 18
John
man
pan
his
when
them

Page 20
teacher's
face
how
reads
story
use
eyes
too

Page 22
Mrs.
King
hold
book
away
from
knows
talks

Page 24
children
moving
sun
shining
keeps
back
window
faces
better

Page 26
teacher
has
put
names
things
classroom
read
that's
right
sink
pencil
sharpener
record
player

Page 28
Camille's
friend
taps
he
him

Page 30
puts
notes
trips
bulletin
board
going
zoo
note
tells
trip
so
forget

Page 32
talk
can't
feel
hand
neck
run
skipping
does
ways
may
sound
seeing
feeling

Page 34
recess
whisper
twins
would
unhappy
missed
was
said

Page 36
uses
pictures
teaches
talking

Page 38
child
should
buddy
show
around
school
playground
running

Page 40
singing
games
just
guess
where
Thumbkin
eensy
weensy
spider

Page 42
looking
work
tired
need
rest

Page 44
always
speak
slowly
fast

Page 46
invite
party
write
invitation
call
telephone
might
want
helps
remember
day
time

Page 48
jump
laugh
harder
smart
aren't
glad
met